First Steps, First Snow

by Harriet Hodgson
illustrated by
Carol Hill Quirk

Published in the United States by BQB Publishing
(an imprint of Boutique of Quality Books Publishing Company)
www.bqbpublishing.com

Printed in the United States of America

978-1-952782-61-9 (hc)
978-1-952782-62-6 (e)

Library of Congress Control Number: 2022935796

Cover and interior illustrations: Carol Hill Quirk
Interior Design Setup: Robin Krauss, www.bookformatters.com
Editor: Andrea Vande Vorde

for all who love forests
and the creatures that
live in them.

iii

iv

1

First steps

in glistening
first snow,

walking just where
I want to go.

4

Not in some stranger's pre-trod track,

5

I wind 'round

and I double back.

Lying down,

arms outstretched

8

like wings.

In the night a lonely
owl sings.

My trail goes through
the white birch wood,

past a stump

where a
tall pine
stood.

Boots poking holes

in crunching snow,

15

still I walk by
the moon's
clear glow.

Shadows of
the timeless
trees

17

and shadow of a cold,
tired me.

18

20

If you have walked by
night you know

the beauty of

first steps,
first snow.

23

24

25

About the Author

Award-winning author **Harriet Hodgson** has a BS in Early Childhood Education from Wheelock College of Education and Human Development at Boston University. She also has an MA in Art Education from the University of Minnesota. After a dozen years in the classroom, Hodgson quit teaching to pursue a writing career. Visit www.harriethodgson.com for more information about this busy mother, grandmother, great-grandmother, author, speaker, doodle artist, and community volunteer.

About the Illustrator

Growing up surrounded by the natural beauty of New England, its classic architecture and rugged landscapes have inspired **Carol Hill Quirk** to draw. With artistic parents who loved to garden, appreciating art and nature was contagious. She majored in Fine Art at Union College in

Schenectady, New York, and then devoted many years to raising her four awesome children. She returned to art with a focus on pen and ink drawings until a friend requested that Carol illustrate *A Letter from Ginger Boy,* which launched her illustrating career.

Her other illustration jobs include: a series of ten books about Sophia the bunny by Judith Johnson Siebold, a series about endangered species named *If We're Gone* by Paige Jaeger, *Janie Presents Philip's Snowman*, and most recently, *Zeus On the Loose.*

28

The Story Behind the Book

First Steps, First Snow is based on a true experience at the family cabin in Wisconsin. Our family had gone to the cabin for the weekend. Snow had been falling most of the day and it finally stopped in the evening.

The difference between the afternoon and night sky was profound. Before, visibility was nil. Now the sky was clear, filled with stars and an unusually bright moon. Our two daughters were asleep when my husband and I decided to go for a walk. We bundled up and stepped outside into a white, frosty, magical world.

We walked amidst pine, birch, and maple trees. Moonlight glistening on snow drifts guided our way. Though we did not see any animals, we knew the forest was filled with them. The poem is a guide for the imagery of walking in the woods. Illustrations take children on the journey and help them identify nocturnal animals.

Walking in fresh snow and making our own path was so memorable I wrote the poem. "First Steps, First Snow," published in the 1983 edition of the *American Poetry Anthology*. The poem is a memory of a wondrous walk at a wondrous time. I hope it helps all readers appreciate nature, forests and the creatures that live there.

Questions to Think About

What do you wear when it gets cold?

Do you have snow boots?

Have you walked in snow at night?

Why didn't the kids bring the dog with them?

What other animals might live in the woods?

Have you made snow angels like the kids in the story?

Do any flowers grow in the forest?

Where would you like your steps to go?